Pam Wedgwood

Grades 0–1

Up-Grade!
Piano Duets

Light relief between the grades

Spaß und Entspannung mit leichten Stücken für Klavierduo Vorstufe
Plaisir et détente avec des pièces simples pour duo pianistique Niveau préliminaire

Contents
page

1	**Close every door**	Rice/Lloyd Webber	2
2	**Sunny side up!**	Wedgwood	4
3	**Greensleeves**	Traditional	6
4	**Sunbeams**	Wedgwood	8
5	**Black-eyed beanie**	Wedgwood	10
6	**Give me joy in my heart**	Anon	12
7	**Over the rainbow**	Harburg/Arlen	14
8	**Roger Rabbit's runaway rag**	Wedgwood	16
9	**The floral dance**	Moss	18
10	**O soldier, soldier**	Traditional	20
11	**Morning**	Grieg	22

ff FABER MUSIC

SECONDO

1. Close every door

Words by Tim Rice
Music by Andrew Lloyd Webber

© 1973 The Really Useful Group Ltd

This music is copyright. Photocopying is ILLEGAL and is THEFT.

PRIMO

1. Close every door

Words by Tim Rice
Music by Andrew Lloyd Webber

© 1973 The Really Useful Group Ltd

PRIMO

2. Sunny side up!

Play this part up an octave

Pam Wedgwood

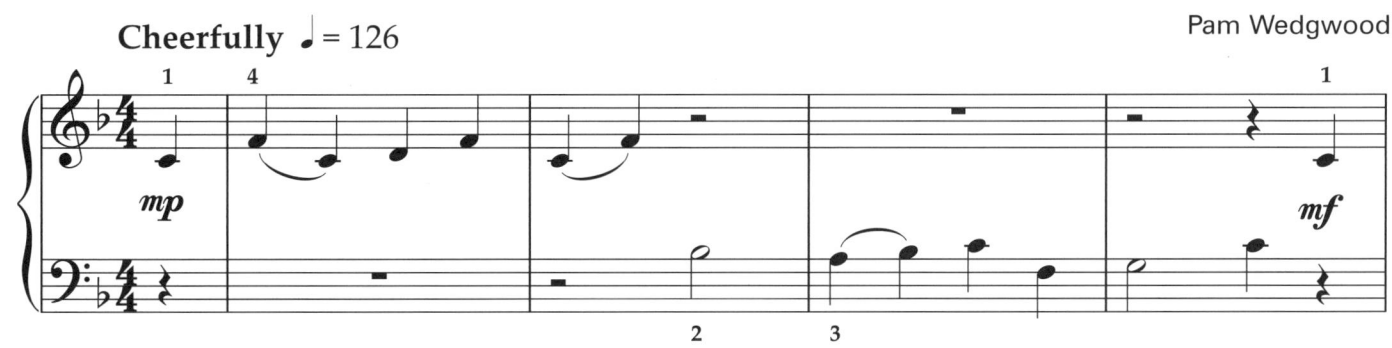
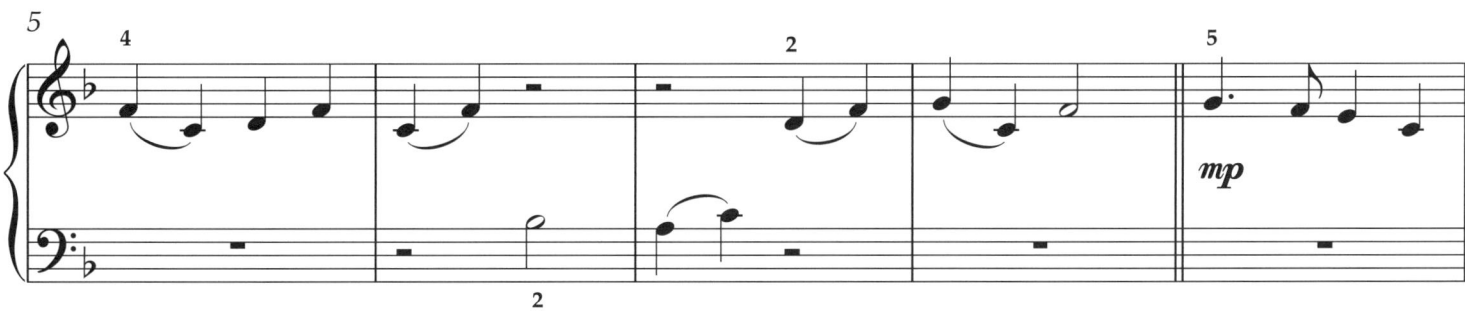
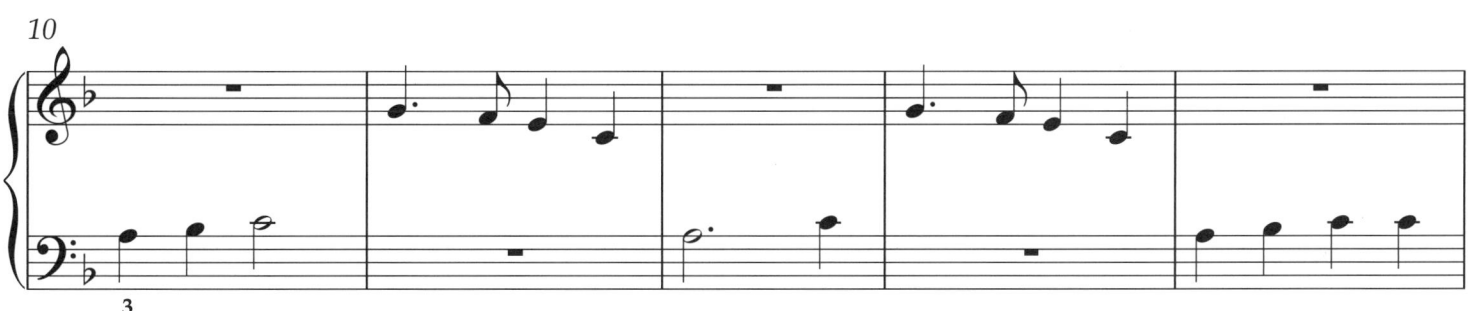

© 2010 by Faber Music Ltd

SECONDO

3. Greensleeves

Traditional

PRIMO

3. Greensleeves

Play this part up an octave

Traditional

© 2010 by Faber Music Ltd

SECONDO
4. Sunbeams

Pam Wedgwood

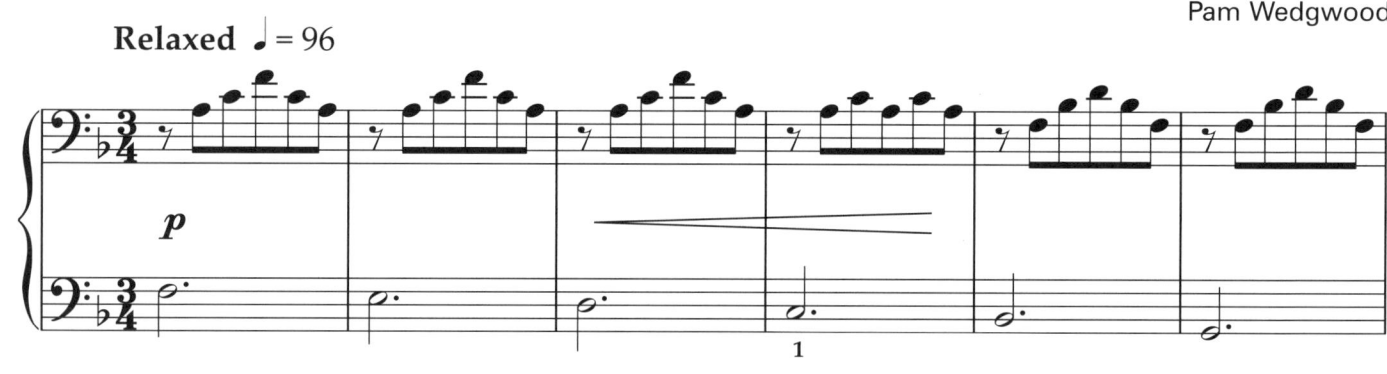
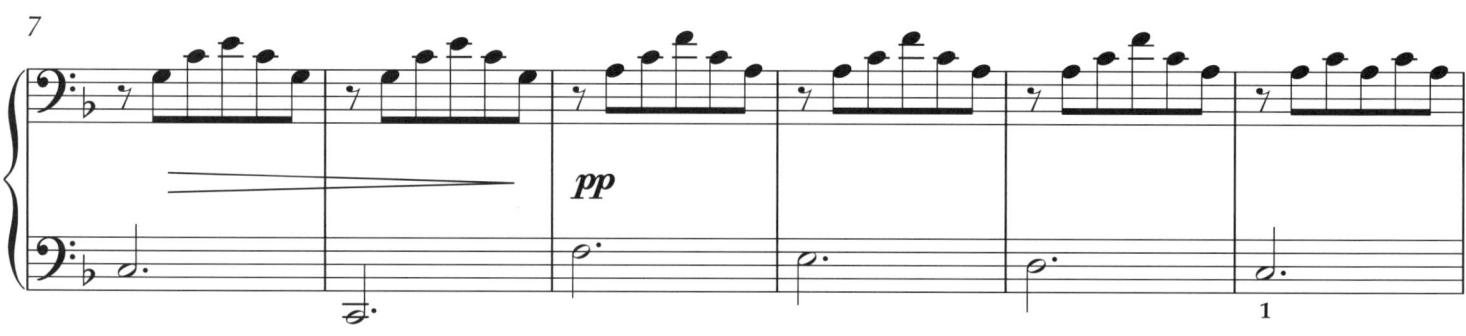

© 2010 by Faber Music Ltd

PRIMO

4. Sunbeams

Play this part up an octave

Pam Wedgwood

SECONDO

5. Black-eyed beanie

Pam Wedgwood

PRIMO

5. Black-eyed beanie

Play this part up an octave

Pam Wedgwood

© 2010 by Faber Music Ltd

6. Give me joy in my heart

SECONDO

Anon.

PRIMO

6. Give me joy in my heart

Play this part up an octave

Anon.

14

SECONDO

7. Over the rainbow

Words by E. Y. Harburg
Music by Harold Arlen

© 1938 EMI Feist Catalog Inc and EMI Catalogue Partnership, EMI United Partnership Ltd (Publishing)
and Alfred Publishing Co (Print) Reproduced by permission. All rights reserved.

16

SECONDO

8. Roger Rabbit's runaway rag

Pam Wedgwood

© 2010 by Faber Music Ltd

PRIMO

8. Roger Rabbit's runaway rag

Play this part up an octave

Pam Wedgwood

SECONDO

9. The floral dance

Words and Music by Katie Moss

© 1911 Chappell Music Ltd.

PRIMO

9. The floral dance

Play this part up an octave

Words and Music by Katie Moss

© 1911 Chappell Music Ltd.

10. O soldier, soldier

SECONDO

Traditional

PRIMO

10. O soldier, soldier

Play this part up an octave

Traditional

PRIMO

11. Morning

Play this part up an octave

Edvard Grieg

 For the online audio played by Pam Wedgwood
scan the QR code or go to:
www.fabermusic.com/content/audio

© 2010 by Faber Music Ltd
This edition © 2018 by Faber Music Ltd
Bloomsbury House
74–77 Great Russell Street
London WC1B 3DA
Music processed by Jeanne Roberts
Cover design by adamhaystudio.com
Printed in England by Caligraving Ltd
All rights reserved

ISBN10: 0-571-53264-0
EAN13: 978-0-571-53264-3

To buy Faber Music publications or to find out about the full range of titles available
please contact your local music retailer or Faber Music sales enquiries:

Faber Music Limited, Burnt Mill, Elizabeth Way, Harlow CM20 2HX
Tel: +44 (0)1279 82 89 82   Fax: +44 (0)1279 82 89 83
sales@fabermusic.com   fabermusicstore.com